CW00544341

Preparing Parent Leaders as Co/Instructors in Higher Learning for Teacher Education

Preparing Parent Leaders as Co/Instructors in Higher Learning for Teacher Education

Mary L. Johnson

Parent U-Turn

INFORMATION AGE PUBLISHING, INC.
Charlotte, NC • www.infoagepub.com

Library of Congress Cataloging-in-Publication Data

A CIP record for this book is available from the Library of Congress
http://www.loc.gov

ISBN: 979-8-88730-355-0 (Paperback)
979-8-88730-356-7 (Hardcover)
979-8-88730-357-4 (E-Book)

Copyright © 2023 Information Age Publishing Inc.

All rights reserved. No part of this publication may be reproduced, stored in a retrieval system, or transmitted, in any form or by any means, electronic, mechanical, photocopying, microfilming, recording or otherwise, without written permission from the publisher.

Printed in the United States of America

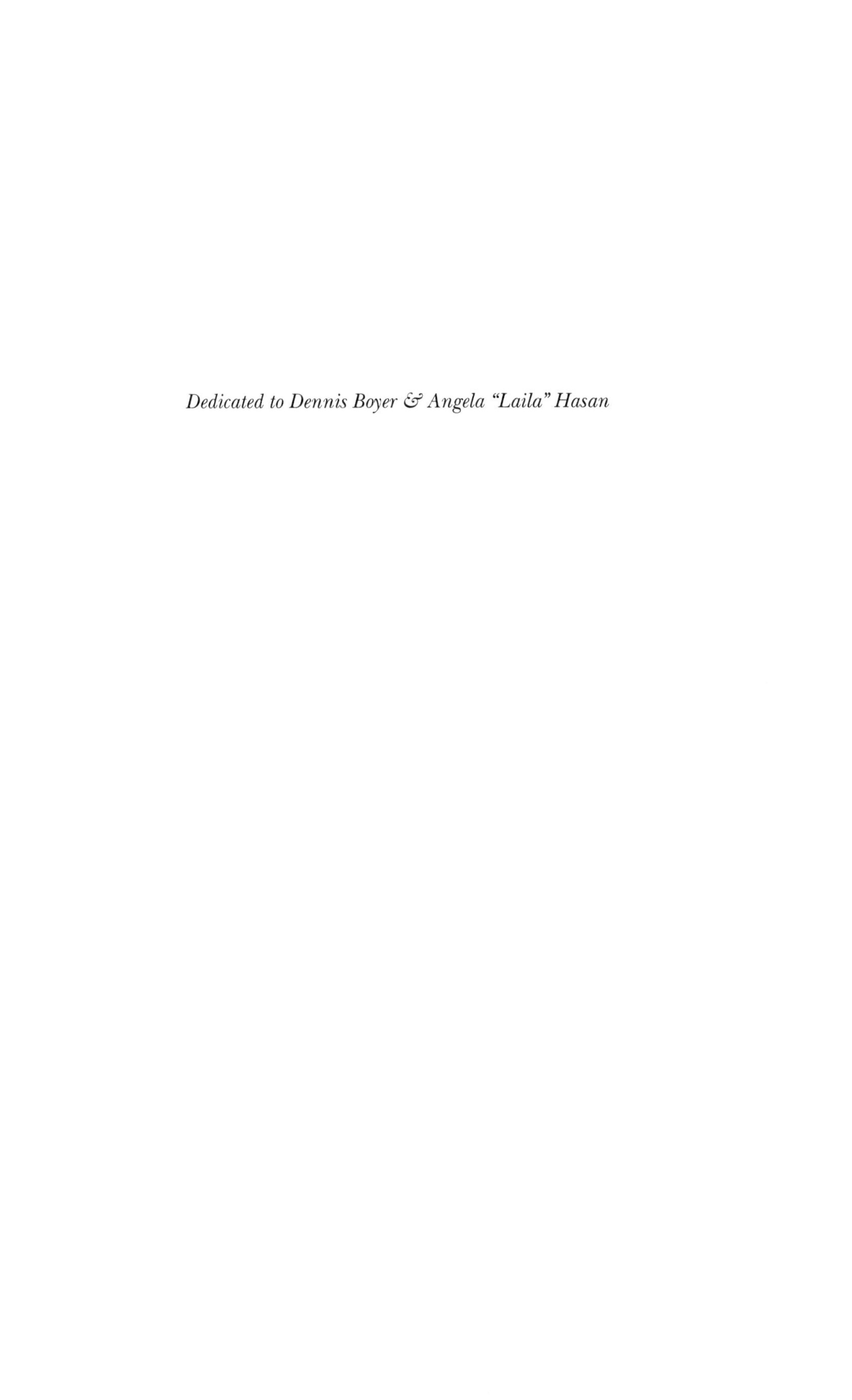

Dedicated to Dennis Boyer & Angela "Laila" Hasan

Contents

Introduction

As a parent advocate and community member having had children of color in the public school system, I needed to think about how I could be involved. This chapter describes how a parent advocate of children from Southeast Los Angeles County has created a distinct approach to parent involvement—an approach that has proven powerful for working-class parents of color who often have no voice in the decisions that most affect their children's learning experiences. It documents a "bottom-up" (rather than top-down) model of accountability that has been effective in getting urban parents of color involved in advocating for their children's and communities' best interests.

Advocating for one's children's educational interests is a time-consuming and demanding task, but a necessary one. As a mother of four children that all attended urban schools in Los Angeles County, I understand that there are many pressing needs and challenges in our neighborhoods. I see the daily distractions and the influences of urban life on low-income children of color that can divert them from their educational obligations. I also see, however, the richness of our neighborhoods in their social networks, diverse languages, the diversity of

Preparing Parent Leaders as Co/Instructors in Higher Learning for Teacher Education, pages 1–2
Copyright © 2023 by Information Age Publishing
www.infoagepub.com
All rights of reproduction in any form reserved.

its population, and the rich multicultural history of our communities. Unfortunately, however, public schools in U.S. urban areas often mirror only the challenges and not the strengths of these communities. They highlight what is wrong with our communities, not what is right. They view our communities as deficient, disadvantaged, and in need of curing, without taking into consideration that schools are here to serve our communities and sometimes it is the school system that needs to be fixed as well.

Researchers have documented the challenges children who attend urban school districts often face and encounter in their academic careers: uncertified teachers, lack of teaching materials (i.e., textbooks), crumbling facilities, low expectations of children of color by school personnel, educator and administrator indifference and apathy, violence, crime, and racial and ethnic tension. The parents and community members of these urban areas, however, don't need researchers to tell us what we already know. What we need are action research tools to document these conditions and organize strategies to change them. Documenting the urban parents' and teachers' experiences is what I and hundreds of other parents have been doing for the last 10 years as parents and community advocates of Los Angeles and as members of Parent U-Turn (PUT), a non-profit organization.

Before the Teacher Preparation Journey

As a parent advocate, I am always pushing for parents' and students' rights and looking to level the playing field on school campuses, so that parents become advocates for their children. Being a parent myself, I always thought that teachers and principals intentionally, willfully, and purposely created a hostile and unfriendly environment, one that pushes parents out of school and similarly, pushes disadvantaged children out. The system makes people feel like they don't belong, or don't fit in. I truly believe that this practice happens so the system can continue its top-down model of thinking that all parents don't care that we as parents don't know what is best for our children. This model of 'deceitful thinking' has been around for decades in schools of color, anywhere the majority of the community is of color and non-white. School leaders generalize that all parents are bad parents and don't care about education. Labeling parents bad allows the system to put the blame for failure on parents.

Working as an advocate I used to think that it was simply 'us' (parents) vs. 'them' (teachers/principals). In my eyes, I was a protector of families and that was the only way I could make changes in the

Preparing Parent Leaders as Co/Instructors in Higher Learning for Teacher Education, pages 3–5
Copyright © 2023 by Information Age Publishing
www.infoagepub.com
All rights of reproduction in any form reserved.

school community. The majority of the school structure was operated according to the top-down model for decades, where parents' and students' voices were treated like second-class citizens in their community schools. Over the years since 2000, I have begun to see or frame the issues from another perspective. Working with Dr. Angela Hasan from the University of California, Los Angeles (UCLA) Parent Project Center X, I started to interact with both teachers and parents. My work with parents was to empower and inspire them to become positive and effective advocates for their children. Parents were trained on how to navigate the Pre-K–16 school structure and curriculum standards. The purposes were to increase parents' awareness of classroom practices and learn how standards are implemented. For example, parents went on a weekly learning walk on the school campus that allowed them to observe teacher instruction while implementing California Learning Standards. After the learning walk was completed, parents and teachers debriefed and discussed among themselves what they had observed. Plus they worked together to find solutions to improve classroom instruction. This method was used to build relations and respect between parents and teachers. This was one of my experiences that helped me change my mindset. I started to believe that there were ways in which we could all get along.

After several years of working with parents at the UCLA Center, I started working with the Teacher Ed Program. The Teacher Ed Program involved the UCLA Parent Project to work with pre-service teachers. The program includes parents as instructors to the pre-service teachers for a day. This program was designed so the pre-service teachers would learn from parents, what parents' expectations are for teachers in our community schools and the roles that parents want teachers to play.

Example 1: In one of the activities, parents assigned teachers as a group to work on a poster called "I AM." Another activity had teachers make a list of roles that the teacher plays in students' lives in an urban school.

Example 2: I am a Teacher, Counselor, etc. After the lists were completed, the pre-service teacher groups presented their posters to all the groups. After all the posters were presented the teachers conducted, a gallery walk showing the posters to parents. While teachers were in their groups doing their assignments, parents came up with the same kind of posters titled, "What I Want From My Child's Teachers."

Example 3: I want my child's teacher to have high expectations for all students. These posters were added to the teachers' poster gallery walk. This way everyone participated in reporting his or her findings to the larger group. Everyone got to walk around and check off ideas and suggestions that they agreed on. The purpose of this exercise was to open up an authentic dialogue up front and confront the "deficit model" that parents and teachers had of each other.

This program went on from 2005 to 2011. Among other outcomes, this allowed pre-service teachers to build relationships and engage with parents outside the book coursework.

The good news is that while working with Center X, I got to meet many professors that impacted my perspective on educational issues. One of these individuals was Rebecca Joseph who taught at Cal State Dominguez Hills. Dr. Joseph expanded our exposure to pre-service teachers outside of UCLA; Cal State Dominguez Hills is located in Carson, California. Dr. Joseph invited me and other parents from my grassroots organization, Parent-U-Turn, to engage with her pre-service teachers at least three or four times a year. We as parents would go into the classroom and sit in a circle with teachers in an open dialogue regarding what is needed for teachers to be successful in urban schools. We were honest and frank as if these prospective teachers were going to be hired in our neighborhood schools.

My Pathway From Advocate to Teacher Education

Never in my wildest dreams did I ever think that I would be an instructor at a major university and teach students working on their Master's degree in the Teacher Education Program. Sometimes I look back and wonder how it happened. Working in Lynwood Unified School District and volunteering in Los Angeles Unified School District, I am well respected among teachers and principals. It is a love-hate relationship. I am beloved by some principals and others see me as a troublemaker. One reason some principals don't like me is that I hold them accountable regarding parents' and students' rights. I guess you might say that I am like a mouthpiece for the parents as a counterbalance to teachers and their unions. As stated, I used to believe that it was "us against them." "Them" were the teachers and principals on the school site. My vision was to empower parents so we could ensure that children would get a better shake. My first experience was at a School Site Council meeting at South Gate High, located in South Gate, California. I heard many stories from parents about how the teachers were

Preparing Parent Leaders as Co/Instructors in Higher Learning for Teacher Education, pages 7–12
Copyright © 2023 by Information Age Publishing
www.infoagepub.com
All rights of reproduction in any form reserved.

misbehaving and I got a first-hand look at them in action. The council was run in a top-down model, where parents who asked questions were immediately, and rudely, shut down. The parents were non-English speakers and the teachers spoke English only. I sat there for 20 minutes until I could no longer stomach the disrespect shown toward my parents. I raised my hand to get recognized to address a question to one of the council members. The chairperson granted my request. I asked the member a question in the same tone of voice in which he had addressed the parents. He turned red and told me I was rude and that he felt insulted; I smiled and responded, "Now you know how the parents are feeling."

Several weeks after the incident I was walking in the hallways at South Gate High School when that same teacher and I crossed each other's paths. I stopped him and asked if I could come and observe his class. He responded "never" as you are not a parent of any of the students in my class. He then complained about me to the principal. What he didn't know is that I had already talked to the principal about parents being a part of learning walks with teachers and principals. The Learning Walk team goes into classrooms to observe class activities, looking for violations of the Williams Settlement case in California. At the end of the learning walk parents and the principal debriefed on what they had seen and how the school could improve. One of the classes that we did observe was that very same art teacher who told me I would never visit his class. This teacher was also the United Teachers Los Angeles (UTLA) chairperson for the teachers' union. He had represented the teachers at the School Site Council (SSC) for 20 years. At every meeting the only thing he did was to push UTLA business, as a result, the meetings were clearly more about adult issues than students' issues, and he put very little effort into working collaboratively. It was just a matter of time before we were going to butt heads like two rams. I just didn't like how he spoke to parents and the community that school year. After 20 years, he stepped away from SSC because he couldn't control the parents anymore. When parents gained their voices, he resigned. We were so delighted that we went out and celebrated. Subsequently, the UTLA membership elected another representative to take his place at SSC.

The new UTLA member that was elected was okay. He spoke to parents in a professional manner and with respect, but his mindset was that all students were bad. Working with this new UTLA representative, the issues discussed were more about students than parents' or teachers' issues. The new member was the dean at the school, which had a high rate of suspension for minor matters such as breaking a pencil in class, or teachers claiming students were looking at a teacher the wrong way. I am very delighted that the principal at the school thought more like me as an advocate for students. I do agree that our School Site Council meeting became more peaceful and friendly than in previous years. The teachers became unhappy with this new representative so he only lasted six months. I truly believe that teachers realized that parents now had a voice in school matters, yet they still wanted to maintain the status quo.

After this most recent UTLA Member stepped down, the previous UTLA President of over twenty years approached me and another parent leader, to inform me that he would like to come back to the School Site Council if we could work together. My response was okay as long as he respects parents' and students' voices as equal partners. We both agreed to work together collaboratively. Over the months, I got to know him and learned more about teacher barriers and challenges. Learning about teachers changed some of my mindset about teachers. In the past, teachers on the School Site Council nominated a teacher to become president of SSC, but to my surprise, the UTLA Chairperson nominated me as president. I asked him why, and he responded that he believed that I would be fair to all stakeholders. I went straight to work on eliminating many of the barriers and challenges of teachers through SSC, such as approval of more supplemental materials for classrooms, intervention programs, field trips, college preparation courses for students, and more support staff for teachers. What I liked was that we would meet in advance to discuss the issues and concerns of all stakeholders. The meetings were always concerning what is needed to benefit students in the classroom. We both agreed that what was good for students was beneficial to teachers as well. In the meetings, he would make the motion and it would be seconded by another member, and then voted on and approved. At the end of that year, I found myself advocating for teachers in the same manner that I advocated for parents and students. I guess you could say that the UTLA Chairperson and I gained a true and authentic parent–teacher collaboration outside the traditional roles. The collaboration started in 2005 and ended in 2012 when I stepped down from SSC at South Gate High.

While I was the President of the LAUSD Parent Collaborative Committee and President of SSC at South Gate High School I attended a UCLA-Institute for Democracy, Education, and Access (IDEA) Summer Institute that was run by Dr. John Rogers and Dr. Jeannie Oakes. We attended the class on the UCLA campus. The summer program was to expose parents and students to researchers and the concept of civil engagement. You could say it was a continuation of the parent training on social justice in 1998 that involved parents in learning about urban education. This was a great gathering of urban students and parents of color collaborating with diverse groups of scholars from UCLA. The seminar taught parents and students how to gather and look at data in our school community. We learned how to document our problems and present the data to the public and elected officials. As parents and students, we gained skills and knowledge that only graduate students experience that are enrolled in the master's program at UCLA. Learning these skills assisted me and others to go back to our school communities and document issues that in the past weren't backed up with data and facts. The first thing we did when we went back to our schools was to document that our students didn't have books or high-quality teachers in the classroom. Survey findings of our schools ended up on the *Los Angeles Times* editorial page. I often think of all the scholars over those summers that shared their knowledge with parents and students; such as Ernest Morrell, Jeff Duncan-Andrade, Angela Hasan, and Anthony Collatos. I will always be grateful to them all.

I got to hang out with most of the scholars and the one that stands out to me because he was in charge of mapping A-G College pathways for our students was Anthony Collatos, a high school teacher and doctoral student who was full of energy and ready to take on the world. He looked like someone from the Brady Bunch and I didn't think that he knew about urban conditions outside of what he had read about us. I wasn't very impressed with him at first, but I later learned not to judge a book by its cover. His passion for outreach and serving the whole family was amazing. Anthony Collatos had a hunger to get students of color to college and was willing to give 110% of himself to that end. He never gave up on the students. Quitting just isn't part of his DNA. After the summer seminar when we saw each other at UCLA events, we would have general conversations. He would mention that parent involvement is the missing ingredient in teacher education programs. As Anthony finished his dissertation, he left UCLA and went to Loyola Marymount University LMU) as a visiting professor. Later on, he contacted me to follow up on his vision of including parents in the Teacher Ed Program.

In 2006 Dr. Collatos became a professor at Pepperdine University and he came up with a pilot program that included parents in the teacher education process-the Urban Parent Teacher Education Collaborative (UPTEC). As mentioned earlier, I first met Dr. Anthony Collatos, aka Tony, at UCLA/IDEA while we were both working with Dr. Jeannie Oakes and Dr. John Rogers. UCLA/IDEA was doing a summer seminar that included parents and students conducting research inquiries and studying civil engagement activities. Every Friday, Dr. Collatos ran the seminar on creating a "College-Going Culture." We had very little contact with each other but we knew of each other's ongoing work. Over the years we became friends. Tony used to invite me and PUT parents to speak with his pre-service teachers at LMU. Dr. Collatos also included me in his work with Teacher for America students and for several years we spoke together on a panel at the Claremont McKenna Graduate School's Teacher Education Program. The feedback on a parent advocate participating with teachers in the program was very positive. Soon, they began requesting me to come and visit more than three times a year. The students would ask Dr. Collatos, "Why can't the parents come more often?"

When Dr. Collatos was hired at Pepperdine University, he continued to include me as a guest speaker twice a year. He came up with a program that consisted of parents, teachers, and students; and he convinced his Dean about the UPTEC program that brought parents and the pre-service teachers together weekly. We became team teachers. The UPTEC program includes the entire missing ingredient in higher education for how to prepare teachers for urban schools. Even though Dr. Collatos and I come from different backgrounds and debate practically everything on how it should be done, our hearts are for social justice and beat as one. In the classroom we are like a married couple, challenging our students to look at all perspectives and not just those presented in books. We get candidates to see that all those theories don't always play out so neatly and tidily in real-life urban or inner-city schools. I usually call it, "The flavor of the month" words and phrases. I truly believe that if a teacher can be successful in urban schools, he/she can teach anywhere.

From an Urban Student to an Urban Teacher—A Narrative

I have so many memories from UPTEC. Every one of them makes me so proud. I feel like the mother of many. Right on the top of my mind, one of my students, Michael, was a very talented and free-spirited individual. Dr. Collatos outreached to Michael all summer to send back his UPTEC application if he was interested in being part of our cohort. No answer all summer. Every student filled out a survey and submitted a short bio. This was our only requirement to be in our cohort. On the first day of class, a young man swaggered in the room donning shorts and flip-flops, and on top of that, he was late. When Dr. Collatos asked him his name, he responded "Michael." Dr. Collatos told him that he wasn't enrolled because he didn't send his application back. Michael told him that he was on vacation without access to a phone. He was a Black male, with a huge ego, and his attitude was that the world owed him something. That night he pushed all of Dr. Collatos' buttons; so much so that Dr. Collatos wanted to drop him from the course. I have seen these behaviors many times in inner-city schools.

Preparing Parent Leaders as Co/Instructors in Higher Learning for Teacher Education, pages 13–15
Copyright © 2023 by Information Age Publishing
www.infoagepub.com
All rights of reproduction in any form reserved.

So I asked Dr. Collatos to allow me to work with Michael. I have seen so many young Black males in high school with a mindset like Michael's. However, I believed Michael could be a great asset to my school community because he would be able to engage with young males that also have a chip on their shoulders. Plus, I liked that Michael did have much respect for his elders.

So, I became the mediator between Dr. Collatos and Michael. I truly believed that I was successful with Michael because I was able to reach this young boy who internally had many fears. He was a long way from home, which was Boston. His parents were very successful educators in higher education, and he was expected to follow in their footsteps. I believe he was afraid that he couldn't measure up. For example, he would befriend females in the cohort to assist him in his coursework, and at times, he even pretended that he was romantically interested. What I liked most about his cohort was they would go to the females and give them a heads-up on Michael's sneaky ways. This showed Dr. Collatos and me that we didn't have to solve everything and that pre-service teachers had developed and fostered their own village.

Michael passed all his necessary tests and then started his student teaching placement. We ended up having to place Michacl at two different school sites. The first placement was in an elementary school in South Gate. There were several challenges and barriers at this school. He was assigned to a predominantly Latino student population and staff. The teachers didn't know how to use Michael's skills. They were using him like he was an errand boy as well as a teacher. They had Michael making copies and serving as a delivery person. He wasn't allowed to observe the collaborative teacher or take over a classroom lesson because he was so busy running non-teaching errands. At first, Michael followed the rules and guidelines that were set by Pepperdine, until he felt that he was being discriminated against because of his skin color. As soon as we got wind of the behavior of the school staff, Dr. Collatos and I quickly removed him. Michael never told us that he was trying to ride it out despite that school not being a good fit for him.

The next big challenge would be keeping Michael focused and not feeling like a victim at his next assigned school. The school he was assigned to was made up of a much more diverse student and staff population. Everything was good for several weeks until I got a call from his master teacher. In the previous school, his master teacher was Latino. At the new school, we placed him with an African-American teacher. She complained that Michael was supposed to be teaching a lesson in the classroom, but instead, he was outside with the children playing basketball—with his shirt off. When she approached him, Michael told her that he needed "his own time out" and immediately went to sit down on the school steps and did nothing. Thank God that his master teacher was from the old school training that knew how to motivate by "tough love." She spoke to Michael in an angry, pissed-off Black mother voice, and demanded that he get back in that classroom. She told him, "You don't have any personal time until school is dismissed." Most teachers would have called the principal and university, and that probably would have ruined Michael's chances of becoming a successful teacher.

Even though Michael was one of my biggest challenges, I never gave up on him. He eventually went on to graduate with his Master's degree and got his teaching credential. He was also the first one from that cohort that received a job that year. His first job as a teacher was in an elite private school in West Los Angeles. In UPTEC he was allowed to stumble and it wasn't held against him, and he was able to overcome his issues until he found himself; a great teacher.

UPTEC South Gate Gallery of Stories

I enjoyed placing teacher education students at South Gate High School (SGHS) in Southeast LA. I had attended SGHS and many of my children graduated from there. I placed over a dozen teacher candidates at SGSH. My greatest memory is hearing the principal over and over requesting from me, "When can we have more Pepperdine teachers?." Even though they were pre-service teachers, they were outshining many of the veteran teachers. The majority of my teachers that completed their pre-service teaching at South Gate High got hired there permanently when they completed their program.

One of the teachers, in her first year, became co-chair of the history department. This same teacher would come up to the parent center during her lunchtime to have her lunch there and build relationships with parents. She would invite me to be the expert in her class when students were doing project-based learning around civic engagement. Other parents were asked to share their experiences as well. She never ate in the teachers' lounge because she wanted to avoid hearing negative comments about parents and students. It makes me so proud to

Preparing Parent Leaders as Co/Instructors in Higher Learning for Teacher Education, pages 17–18
Copyright © 2023 by Information Age Publishing
www.infoagepub.com
All rights of reproduction in any form reserved.

see pre-service teachers actually implementing strategies that were taught in the UPTEC program.

Another pre-service teacher from Pepperdine that taught English was hired as a permanent teacher. In her second year, her students scored the highest in the school on the California Standards Test. She also headed up the school newsletter and the principal used her to mentor some of the veteran teachers. Yes, she was young but teaching came easy for her. She demanded respect from her students even though she was the same age as many of her students' sisters or brothers at home.

Since many of the student teachers are young, they sometimes face the challenge of students flirting with them inappropriately. One of our pre-service teachers faced that issue. She was a science teacher at the school and one of her male students made a "sexy" remark toward her. She immediately sent him to the dean and told him that the young man couldn't come back to her class until his parents came to a meeting with her. She used UPTEC strategies regarding classroom management by setting a standard. Plus, she demanded a written apology and a meeting with the parents to discuss the student's lack of respect and the fact that proper behavior was expected.

Beyond Teacher Preparation: The Urban Parent Teacher Education Collaborative

The Urban Parent Teacher Education Collaborative (UPTEC) is a pioneering model for other universities. By creating a space for a university professor and a grass-roots parent organizer to team teach a class for pre-service teachers, institutions of higher learning in California such as Pepperdine University are beginning to recognize parents as experts in areas concerning how and what is needed to educate children in urban schools. UPTEC allows future teachers to have contact with urban parents before they come into our school communities. In workshops, pre-service teachers are given strategies for interacting with parents to learn how to build a working relationship with them. Parent-U-Turn members and teachers, for example, practice role reversals that allow both teachers and parents to acquire a better understanding and respect for the importance of each other's roles.

Preparing Parent Leaders as Co/Instructors in Higher Learning for Teacher Education, pages 19–22
Copyright © 2023 by Information Age Publishing
www.infoagepub.com
All rights of reproduction in any form reserved.

What makes UPTEC unique is that teacher education students self-select to participate in it. The students are with a university professor and a parent advocate for a yearlong program. UPTEC is a community-based model of teacher education that includes urban parents in a pre-service teacher education program. Originally, it was a three-part teacher education course developed and co-taught by Dr. Anthony Collatos and myself. It was funded initially by a Faculty Service Award grant. It was also a two-year research project that sought to understand how pre-service teachers' engagement in the program influenced their perceptions of urban schools and communities; how they include parents and communities in their classrooms; and how their identities as urban educators were formed. The educational community, for the first time, was gathering empirically based data for more community-based teacher education programs.

Our students get to learn about urban schools with guidance from a grass-roots parent that lives in the community that most students have only read about in a book. With the help of Dr. Collatos, we can bring the reality of urban schooling to the classroom. In most institutes of higher learning the students get limited exposure to parents and students before they are placed in urban communities. At UPTEC, we pride ourselves in preparing our students for the everyday conditions and barriers that our teachers will encounter. Before we place pre-service teachers in a community, we take them on a tour of that school and community. This is done to alleviate some of the fears and stereotypes of a given neighborhood. It is very important to us that pre-service teachers feel safe and comfortable in their new environment before placement. Plus, we meet with master teachers and interview them to identify the right fit. Some veteran teachers are good at what they do, but not good at nurturing and guiding pre-service teachers. So, the master teacher must be willing to share her or his classroom with pre-service teachers. The master teacher can make positive or negative experiences for teacher candidates. Our goals in UPTEC are to ensure that our students from our cohorts have positive experiences. Dr. Collatos and I make many visits to the local LAUSD schools to ensure our students' teachers are working in their job descriptions. The first thing Dr. Collatos and I tell the students is, "Yes, you are a part of Pepperdine, and you also belong to something bigger, which is UPTEC." Once you are enrolled in UPTEC, you are part of the UPTEC village for a lifetime. The village comes with benefits which means we help future cohorts to navigate Pepperdine Teacher Ed Program and to find jobs when they graduate.

Even after graduation, past cohorts come back to visit. UPTEC alums often present to current cohorts and speak to these new candidates about their teaching experiences and matters related to the workplace and what they will face upon graduation. In April and May of each year, our employed UPTEC teachers send out information for possible teaching positions available at their schools. Also every year Dr. Collatos hosts a get-together where you have individuals from all cohorts come together. We all come from different backgrounds, some from urban or rural settings, some from working-class parents, and others from upper and middle-class families. The dedication and commitment to engage urban students and parents are equal across socio-economic classes.

Example: There was one student teacher whose parents didn't want her to work in an urban school, even though her parents owned a business in a similar urban community. This student teacher would cry while driving into the school. My advice to her was to invite her parents to attend the back-to-school night that was coming up soon. Not only did they come, but they fell in love with the students and their parents. Subsequently, they came back on another day, cooked for the whole class, and would volunteer in the class.

Every candidate for UPTEC must write an application essay about themselves and why they want to teach in urban schools. This method is used for us to get to know the candidate before the program starts. UPTEC has never turned away any candidates that applied merely because of the essay. The most fun part of recruitment is that our current and previous cohorts are a part of the process. They email the possible candidate on our behalf and join Dr. Collatos and me when we go out to recruit students at different forums. It is amazing to hear the students talk about their experiences in UPTEC. Our UPTEC cohorts are our biggest cheerleaders and supporters and have energized our base of cohorts over the years. Many people talk about the "village" but truly our cohort is "their brothers' and sisters' keeper." If you are ever on Facebook, the picture I have as my profile is from the first cohort. Also on social media, you see postings by individuals from many previous cohorts. Even though many of our previous students have moved away, they maintain contact through social media and frequently attend each other's parties and weddings. For example: One of our cohort members got married in Maine and she wanted the entire cohort to attend so she paid all travel and lodging expenses for them to share the moment with her.

The UPTEC model of teacher education seeks to build a clinical laboratory for prospective teachers to acquire skills to work with parents and communities. I believe that one of the main reasons UPTEC works is because of Dr. Collatos. He has much experience working with urban youth and families. In many instances, a university professor and a grass-roots advocate wouldn't be a good combination. Dr. Collatos' experiences working with students of color are extra resources in preparation for our new teachers regarding high expectations for all students in urban schools. We both bring this knowledge and experience to share in the preparation of future teachers on how to navigate conditions and barriers that are not written about in books but exist in urban schools.

For example: One day we played out different scenarios that might happen in inner-city schools dealing with parents and students. I wrote out different scenarios for the cohort students and their roles. Some of the teachers had anxiety about not having a script and of having not practiced before they had to play out the part. I explained to them that in urban schools, you won't have time to problem-solve before incidents happen and you must be flexible and roll with the flow. One student teacher was so upset and nervous that she freaked out in fear. Her scenario was how she would handle an upset parent that was aggressive in her body language. I believe that this exercise was the beginning of a change of mindset for this individual that had many stereotypical images of urban parents. Because of exposure to these kinds of activities, this individual is now in her third year as a permanent teacher in an urban school. I am proud to report that UPTEC continues to work with parents and advocates on their behalf.

Increase Teachers' Skillset and Positive Attitudes Toward Urban Families

Our student teachers must have as much experience reaching out to families during their placements at schools. For example, we host some graduate classes in parent centers at local school sites. Plus, we get local parents to come in and interview the cohorts on why they want to be teachers. Parents also share their expectations for their children and all children in urban schools. In many cases, this is the first time that student teachers have engaged with parents in discussions on what they expect from teachers. Several teachers have lunch with parents when they are placed at a school site. Also, several teachers use the parent center as a hub for community projects involving their students. Parents are asked to come to class and speak to students on different topics that affect the school community. This was the first time that teachers used parents as experts (i.e., relatives of their own K–12 students). In the past parents were only asked to be chaperones. I was very happy that UPTEC student teachers started a new tradition

Preparing Parent Leaders as Co/Instructors in Higher Learning for Teacher Education, pages 23–24
Copyright © 2023 by Information Age Publishing
www.infoagepub.com
All rights of reproduction in any form reserved.

that other teachers could soon follow, engaging parents as partners in their children's education.

UPTEC gives the pre-service teachers a sense of belonging. We share knowledge of the school structure and budgets that fund schools. Our students learn to navigate the school structure so they won't be overwhelmed. Teachers are taught about things such as Title 1 funds, and how to request funds for supplemental materials and buses for school trips. Plus, they attend School Site Councils, Title 1 Councils, and English Learner Councils so they experience the process in person and not just what they learn in the cohort. After many years, many UPTEC alums are a part of the decision-making teams (School Site Councils, ELAC, and Title 1) at their school sites.

Beyond classroom-based teaching methods that offer teachers direct field experiences working with families, student teachers are also required to participate in a community project while they are doing their pre-service. One cohort of students developed a needs assessment and a project for the school that was not provided by schools such as an elementary science lab, language lab, and a college access lab. It is required by UPTEC that our student teachers must go beyond the teacher's normal duties and classes. For examplc, many of our student teachers volunteer for community events such as Family Day in the Park. This is where everyone comes together in a community to serve families in areas of health care, safety, and education. One year, our cohort volunteers read to students and families at the Annual Christmas Posada Celebration. After the Posada, our pre-service teachers gave away books and tamales to families. Dr. Collatos and I try to ensure a proper balance between community activities and classroom efforts. We truly believe that our cohorts must go among the families where they live if they are going to build a relationship with them. The parents get to see their teachers outside the classroom and teachers get to speak with parents without any pressure. So, celebration events are good arenas to break the ice and bridge lines of communication.

Develop Effective Practices That Prepare Teachers to Work With Families

We believe that effective practice can only be developed through experiences. The first thing is working with student teachers on getting rid of stereotypes/myths. We always place two to three student teachers on a school site together for support. Also, we assign student teachers with master teachers that have a history of working with families. When first assigned student teachers check out the school and speak to the principal about different roles that teachers are expected to do at his or her school. We also try to place student teachers with past alumni of the university who were prepared in our program. These are some examples of practices and strategies to work successfully with families and communities:

- Use examples and show parents how to use shortcuts in textbooks, conduct workshops, strategies, and writing skills; encourage parents to use the library as a resource.
- Work together to help students

Preparing Parent Leaders as Co/Instructors in Higher Learning for Teacher Education, pages 25–26
Copyright © 2023 by Information Age Publishing
www.infoagepub.com
All rights of reproduction in any form reserved.

- Know what's going on in students' homes
- Find opportunities to get to know parents
- Open up communication, listen to parent concerns
- Learn about the community
- Parents are a fountain of cultural knowledge and encouragement

Establish a Context for Teachers to Learn About Urban Communities

The first thing is to help teacher education students who haven't lived in an urban community to get rid of their fears. For a student who has no experience working with children and families of color, it can be a cultural shock. This is why you start slowly to break down misconceptions and stereotypes.

Example: Do activities that make student teachers reflect on their beliefs with their peers. Write down the barriers and conditions that parents and students in non-urban schools might face and then compare them to the same conditions and barriers that teachers in urban schools might have. Both groups' outcomes are similar and afterward, students write down in reflections, what would be some of the solutions for barriers and conditions.

Why Am I here?

- Talk about parents' expectations of children/students
- Issues encountered in the classroom

Preparing Parent Leaders as Co/Instructors in Higher Learning for Teacher Education, pages 27–29
Copyright © 2023 by Information Age Publishing
www.infoagepub.com
All rights of reproduction in any form reserved.

- Talk about issues in the community; how these affect students; how teachers can help students to learn
- Caring parent
- Parents' concerns about behavior issues vs. academic issues
- Find out what's beautiful
- Learn how to build better relationships with parents

Another example: Let the student teachers shadow a parent for a day. The cohort is exposed to the community by eating in their neighborhood and/or volunteering at community events. Parents are ambassadors for the students' teachers in the community. This is the only way the teacher can learn about culture and barriers that contribute to the myth that parents don't care. There are some books that the university uses that give insight into social and cultural issues, but at the end of the day, only real experiences in urban schools can build that knowledge.

Increase working relationships between novice teachers and families and students that break down perceptions of stereotypes and improve student achievement. Pair up the teacher with parents to attend different events such as literacy, math, and back-to-school night. This allows teachers and parents to be seen as experts working together in collaboration for student achievement. This shows parents that their knowledge is valuable and respected. We encourage our student teachers to write notes to parents introducing themselves as the teacher and thanking the parents for sending their children to the school. These are the kinds of things that can generate trust and build relationships. Communication in multicultural and multilingual communities accepts and promotes languages that parents speak in their homes. Communication between home and school must not only be a regular, two-way occurrence; it also has to be relevant and meaningful. Over and over I share with novice teachers to smile a lot and greet their students at the classroom door. When possible, invite parents to their classroom and make meetings with parents when it is convenient to the parents. If parents don't come to you, then find a peer and make a home visit. The students will then know that you will do anything to help them improve. Plus, the parents will know that you are serious about their child's education. For UPTEC, the schools are part of the community and parents are the core of the community in assuring friendly and supportive services for their children. These are some examples of strategies that help to increase trust and respect among teachers and parents:

- Find out expectations for children in this neighborhood
- Build relationships with parents and teachers
- Build capacity by talking to parents at parent centers, PTAs, and other gatherings (e.g., Parent Advisory Councils)
- Build relationships with parents EARLY
- Involve parents
- Be creative in running your classes
- Literacy: take different approaches to have kids practice reading in situations that aren't embarrassing
- Classroom management: take control of your classroom
- Bring behavioral issues to the attention of parents and be consistent in getting children to help with issues
- Make personal connections with students

Challenges and Barriers to Educational Reform

A challenge to teachers in preparation is regarding social justice, what it is, and does it exist. The phrase "social justice" is spoken a lot in higher education. Social justice has so many meanings depending on the professor or individual who is trying to make a point about urban education. So, pre-service programs must know how to interpret the usage of the word, so they are agents of change. In our cohorts, Dr. Collatos explains the scholar's definition and I discuss the reality of what parents want from social justice.

Our teachers must learn that social justice doesn't just mean changing the system without academics as the first priority. If a child masters academic success, they can advocate for themselves. In many cases student teachers have advocated for changes involving restrooms and cafeteria food; but very little about curriculum instruction and safety. This is one reason that Dr. Collatos and I have our students doing community work in the urban neighborhood so they can have a reality check. The reality check lets the teachers determine and reflect

Preparing Parent Leaders as Co/Instructors in Higher Learning for Teacher Education, pages 31–33
Copyright © 2023 by Information Age Publishing
www.infoagepub.com
All rights of reproduction in any form reserved.

on what social justice means to them. My observation and discussion with pre-service teachers often reveal that the reality of the curriculum and instruction in urban students in their classes is a major difference from the curriculum and instruction in K–12 schools in the suburbs. For example, one of our students that had a placement in an elementary school was very frustrated with the quality of education for first graders. That perception came because the student teacher was comparing her first-grade education in a non-urban school with what she was seeing in her inner city, urban school. The difference, of course, was vast and shocking to her. For example, her students did not recognize sight words or even their ABCs. In California Preschool or Kindergarten are not required.

In another example, there was a lockdown at school, no one could come onto campus, and no one could leave. There are plenty of lockdowns in the inner-city schools, and suburban schools as well. This method of security is employed as a precaution when there is a possible danger around the school site. This action causes anxiety for our student teachers because many of them have never had these kinds of experiences in their formal education or community. If our cohort or any new teacher is going to survive in urban schools (aka inner city schools), they must have these kinds of experiences before becoming certificated teachers. These experiences allow the pre-service teachers to reflect before committing to inner-city schools. The reality hits them that there is a two-tiered school system, suburban and urban, and that each runs differently. One system is more organized and the other can seem dysfunctional at best. In the latter case, from day to day, things are different and exciting if you can be flexible. It is our job in higher learning to prepare our teachers for both urban and suburban schools. We must remember that there are no magic bullets and that one model of teaching doesn't fix all schools or the students that attend them.

The main problem with teacher preparation programs is that they are using a "one model fits all approach." The university has not moved into the 21st century and the world of reality with its course offerings. Most novice teachers follow the examples of individuals who taught them. For example, a male pre-service teacher teaches his students like they are in college classes. The problem with this is that these students have never experienced this kind of lecture environment and he wonders why his students weren't getting it. One UPTEC teacher wanted to leave teaching because he felt unappreciated by the students. This is where Dr. Collatos and I intervened and mentored him about strategies and unreal expectations, as well as about changing his lesson plan and delivery styles. What we like is that our teachers are reflecting and not blaming the children. By reflecting, they are constantly changing to fit the children that they are serving. You see, social justice isn't just about the students you serve, it is also about teachers who are serving them by doing everything possible to create the right environment. This kind of environment can only happen when our teachers learn how our children learn and not how the teachers want them to learn. Textbooks are not the only way to promote learning and sadly, this is the method typically found in higher education. In our cohort, our novice teachers get exposure to special education, English learners, and disadvantaged students on how they learn and barriers/conditions that might affect classroom learning.

Universities still want to do their training of teachers based on 19th and 20th century models. Those models were considered good for that time but not for the 21st century and not in inner-city schools. The 21st century is about technology and there is very little training engaging pre-service teachers on how to use technology in the classroom other than using smart boards and whiteboards. We should be preparing our young teachers to use things that interest their students such as digital resources and texting. We need to incorporate these things as a normal part of students' classroom work. Most schools have rules against these items because of a lack of exposure to higher education and training on how to create a positive environment in the classrooms. It is hard to put teacher educators outside their comfort zone relative to how they were trained and how they learned. These are the same individuals preparing our 21st century teachers, but they are limited in skills that are needed for the 21st century. I feel that lifelong learning is a phrase that people in higher education echo but truly don't know what that means. It should mean that individuals continue to update their skills to be effective as society changes.

UPTEC's Contributions

In this section, I describe how UPTEC has contributed to multiple stakeholder communities.

For Students

UPTEC helped develop "community teachers" (Murrell, 2001) and increased candidates' cultural competence and ability to work with urban families.

For Faculty

UPTEC increased the teacher education program's access to Parent U-Turn. Their presence on campus and in the classroom provided the education faculty with the opportunity to work with urban parents and to understand the social, cultural, and political contexts of urban communities.

Preparing Parent Leaders as Co/Instructors in Higher Learning for Teacher Education, pages 35–36
Copyright © 2023 by Information Age Publishing
www.infoagepub.com
All rights of reproduction in any form reserved.

For Higher Education

The partnership with urban parents added critical community knowledge to the teacher education program and solidified the university's presence in urban communities.

For Pepperdine University

This relationship increased the university's profile with groups serving the most under-resourced communities and provided a model for teacher education programs across the nation. In addition, this model of teacher education can also inform other teacher education programs and provide opportunities for other collaborations.

For the Community at Large

The program's collaborative efforts to include students and families in the teacher education process provided a model for school-community partnerships and informed state (SB-2042) and national (ESSA) policies.

Seven Steps for Survival for First-Year Urban Teachers

All educators are facing new pressures that make it more crucial than ever for new teachers to learn the strategies and methods that make for higher quality instruction and build school bridges and capacity for a successful tomorrow.

Step 1—Engage with your students' families. Use examples and show parents how to use shortcuts in textbooks, give workshops, strategies, and skills; invite parents to the library and your classroom.

Step 2—Work together to help students. Teachers & parents both need to compromise and set goals together so that they're on the same level to find out about the child's strengths and weaknesses.

Step 3—Know what's going on in the student's house. Teachers need to bridge a connection and network with families, community,

Preparing Parent Leaders as Co/Instructors in Higher Learning for Teacher Education, pages 37–38
Copyright © 2023 by Information Age Publishing
www.infoagepub.com
All rights of reproduction in any form reserved.

and students in the school community. Higher participation results/volunteers

Step 4—Find opportunities to get to know parents. Teachers must communicate to parents when students are performing well, not just when problems arise.

Step 5—Open up communication, and listen to parents' concerns. Address parents' concerns head-on. If you are taking an action that raises questions, work to show parents the benefits of your methods and explain your reasoning to them. There must be multiple ways to communicate with parents besides just "handouts, flyers" (e.g., home visits).

Step 6—Learn about the community. Teachers need to move beyond stereotypes that may be grounded in their own perspective frame of deceit models or myths about "good families." Community field trip day/BBQ; trash day; litter pick up day; improve the community day.

Step 7—Parents are a fountain of cultural knowledge and encouragement. Teachers also need to identify non-threatening opportunities to welcome parents with diverse backgrounds to the school. Attending community gatherings and traditional events is one way to do this.

What Every Parent Wishes Teachers Knew

Here are the best practices that parents wish teachers knew. Over the years, these are the most important items that parents have shared with me about how teachers could best work with our children.

1. *Happy parents make happy teachers.* Keeping parents happy is an extra assignment for teachers that does come with consequences. Unhappy parents can be barriers to teachers because of a lack of communication and dialogue around students' academic progress. Parents of urban students have various resources and experiences with schools. Some teachers have positive and some have negative experiences as students themselves or engaging with school staff. The need to please parents should be reflected constantly in every teacher's thinking. We as parents think teachers should be perfect and are the experts because they have an education degree.
2. *All veteran teachers are the best teachers.* Parents have to cross their fingers wishing their child wouldn't get a veteran teacher that hasn't updated his/her skills to engage students with 21st-

Preparing Parent Leaders as Co/Instructors in Higher Learning for Teacher Education, pages 39–41
Copyright © 2023 by Information Age Publishing
www.infoagepub.com
All rights of reproduction in any form reserved.

century teaching/learning methods. As a parent I felt nervous the night before my school year began, hoping and praying that my child would get a teacher that was prepared to take them to a new level of learning. I just wanted a newbie or veteran teacher that could create an environment where students would be happy and inspire them to learn. It was never important to me how long they were a teacher but how they could inspire and motivate learning. All teachers, newbies or veterans, must earn parents' and community's trust. We as parents don't just give people the benefit of the doubt, "You must earn it."

3. *Old ways of learning versus new ways of teaching.* Many Students in the 21st century are taught differently from how their parents were taught. Many parents think like teachers, that is, "It worked for me and I learned and am uncomfortable with changes." We as parents and teachers are always comparing how it was when we were students attending school. Parents wish teachers would stay with the status quo more and less with changes. "Sometimes it's hard for teachers to understand that we need to gradually change the environment, this allows us to adjust and see the bigger picture for our students.
4. *It's okay for kids to fail.* Parents don't want kids to fail, because they believe it is a reflection on them as parents. Yet we know that if our child doesn't try, he/she has already failed. Every parent prays before seeing his/her child's report card that there are no Fs. Society may think as parents you must not have helped your child enough or supported them in their learning, that something went wrong at home and not in the classroom. We don't want teachers to have pity for our children but rather to hold them to high expectations and push them to be all they can be, and if they fail they will get up and do it again. It is like riding a bike. In the beginning, you fall but you keep on trying and after a while, you eventually ride without falling. We as parents want teachers to know that we want our children to earn the grades they get, and that grades must not be a result of sympathy for the child/ren.
5. *Be a good listener.* It can be hard for teachers to hear that their child is having a social or academic problem because they don't know the challenges and barriers of the community they

are teaching in. I urge teachers to get to know the people in their school community. Know that every child and adult, myself as well, has life challenges that will impact the student's learning. It should never come down to thinking that "it's teachers against parents." Many times, it becomes a battle and the only loser is the student. We must work together to benefit the child's academic success.

6. *Our child's homework reinforces what is learned.* We wish that teachers understand that they're no more *Leave It to Beaver* families in certain communities, where the mother stays home and fathers go to work. Homework is something that a child did in school and came home to do reinforcement of that learning. That is not how it is playing out at home in inner-city schools. Most children come home with no understanding of the assignment and the parents have to take hours to reteach some things that the child should have already known of. It is not an excuse that parents who might be working two jobs just to make ends meet can't or don't have the time to reteach something that should have been learned within that school day. It is not good modeling or good acceptance of responsibility to hear teachers pass the blame to parents as to why their child didn't do their homework
7. *Stay engaged and involved after school hours.* Teachers want to schedule back-to-school nights on teachers' times and not convenient for parents. Most back-to-school nights in my community run from 3 p.m. to 5 p.m. Other school events are scheduled around when the teacher is available, not the parents. The word night should be the keyword to engage parents. Parents work to make a living and most individuals don't get off work until 5 p.m. or later. The meeting should be scheduled in the evening from 6 p.m. to 7:30 p.m. if you really want to engage parents. I always wonder what if the meeting were held on Saturday, who would attend? I would put my money on parents and a limited number of teachers. If meetings are tailored to when the community is available and that is most likely well after school hours you will get a greater turnout. You must meet the parents and community halfway. I urge teachers to meet or call parents before progress report or report card time.

UPTEC Preserve Teacher Testimonials

These are reflections from previous UPTEC teachers about their experiences and journey throughout the UPTEC program.

The UPTEC Journey

Aimee Lopez, UPTEC Alumni, Pepperdine University

> My experience with the Urban Parent Teacher Education Collaborative became more than an academic one but granted me the support I needed to persevere over self-doubt, tap into my resiliency, and use my passion for education to help others do the same.

Parent Advocates Influence Me as a Teacher

Mayanthi Imbuldeniya, UPTEC Alumni, Pepperdine University

> I believe that being a member of UPTEC was the greatest benefit of attending Pepperdine. In particular, having Mary Johnson as a

Preparing Parent Leaders as Co/Instructors in Higher Learning for Teacher Education, pages 43–45
Copyright © 2023 by Information Age Publishing
www.infoagepub.com
All rights of reproduction in any form reserved.

co-teacher of the class. If I had not become one of Mary's students, I would have never known the most valuable resource I have to educate children are their parents and caregivers. I would have continued to subscribe to my belief that the parents of urban youth simply do not care (a sentiment that I even still hear teachers sharing in the lunchroom).

Journey to Becoming a Community Teacher

Emmanuel Aguiar, UPTEC Alumni-Pepperdine University

Pepperdine's UPTEC program offered the social justice component as well as the ability to return to the community where I grew up to do my student teaching. I developed a critical perspective through the years at UCLA and at the time I received an opportunity to put into action my ideas about teaching that would be fueled more so by UPTEC's social justice component as well as contribute to my community, giving me a rich experience as opposed than student teaching at a different.

Quartney Cervantes, UPTEC Alumni–Pepperdine University

Much of my ideas and support while finding my way came from UPTEC and with the support of UPTEC. As I am growing as an educator and individual, I remind myself every day that I found a way to do what I love and what I am passionate about.

My Journey From Community Organizer to Becoming Urban Teacher

Ray Tellez, UPTEC Alumni-Pepperdine University

As a member of UPTEC, we held classes in the parent center. Mary helped me see that if teachers are willing to listen to parents, there can be true parent–teacher collaboration. As part of the program, we met with parents from Parent-U-Turn—a nonprofit student and parent advocacy group that worked in local area schools and had children that attended the schools where the UPTEC students were placed. As I listened to these parents, I was reminded of my own mother.

Parent Leaders Testimonial

Parent leaders and advocates were essential to the UPTEC program. Here are several testimonials from the parent leader experiences.

Valerie Munoz, PUT

> It was an honor to go to Pepperdine University to speak to teachers that wanted to gain knowledge from a parent and the community. These same teachers do community projects at the local school where they are doing their internship.

Juan Godine, Parent Advocate

> It was awesome that parents were able to advocate for jobs in our local schools. The principal asked the parents, "Can you please send more Pepperdine University Teachers to their schools?" Their student teachers became department chairs, football coaches, and School Site Presidents.

Conclusion

It has been my great honor to be able to work with preservice. It was the eagerness to learn from parents and the community. It was so great to see the growth of the students' teachers. Their schedules were heavy with coursework, yet they were committed to getting on the freeway and driving to a community miles away from Pepperdine University and their homes. Many of these pre-service teachers have never been to inner-city communities. I learn from them the preservice too, that parents and teachers can come together when there is mutual respect for one another. Pepperdine University's teacher education model ensures parents as equal partners in this collaborative work. The dean and other professors treated me and other parents as experts and as equals. Parents were invited to subcommittee meetings to give feedback on the upcoming program and curriculum. Higher education treated us parents differently than our local school. Our school never invited parents to attend professional development with teachers.

I would also like to thank Dr. John Rogers and Dr. Susan Auerbach for their feedback and support while writing this book.

Preparing Parent Leaders as Co/Instructors in Higher Learning for Teacher Education, pages 47–48
Copyright © 2023 by Information Age Publishing
www.infoagepub.com
All rights of reproduction in any form reserved.

In closing, I would like to thank Dr. Anthony Collatos for believing in this concept of having a parent advocate as a co-instructor and bringing parents' experience into a year-long program. We were able to bring to the preservice teachers both book learning and real-life experiences from the parents and families of their urban students. These parents still dream and have insights on how to change inner-city schools. Thank you Pepperdine University and Dr. Collatos for the most amazing journey and for being the pioneer in this model.

* * *

Anthony Collatos, PhD, Professor of Education, Pepperdine University. Dr. Collatos' research interests include the sociology of education, critical research, urban education, teacher education, college access pathways, equitable learning opportunities, and school/community partnerships. Dr. Collatos directs multiple projects including the Urban Parent Teacher Education Collaborative (UPTEC), the Pat Lucas Center for Teacher Preparation, and the Teaching and Learning in an Age of COVID-19 study. These projects work with students, families, teachers, and educational leaders throughout the educational pipeline. He has published multiple articles and manuscripts and regularly presents his research locally, nationally, and internationally. Dr. Collatos is also a former school board member and has taught middle and high school social studies, and coached and mentored youth. He has a PhD from the University of California, Los Angeles.

About the Author

Mary L. Johnson is the founder and director of Parent U-Turn—a non-profit committed to providing educational training, research, and advocacy for students and their families. As the CEO of Parent-U-Turn, Mary has over 30 years of experience advocating for local, national, and state parent engagement. Mary Johnson is a practitioner who has developed the seven advocacy standards for urban and rural parents and teachers that successfully help parents and teachers navigate their children through low-performing urban and rural schools and higher education.

Preparing Parent Leaders as Co/Instructors in Higher Learning for Teacher Education, page 49
Copyright © 2023 by Information Age Publishing
www.infoagepub.com
All rights of reproduction in any form reserved.

Milton Keynes UK
Ingram Content Group UK Ltd.
UKHW021956290923
429673UK00005B/161